Follow 52

Following the 52 commands of Jesus one command and one week at a time

By Joel Holm

ISBN: 0986181951
ISBN-13: 9780986181955

DEDICATION

To Jesus

CONTENTS

ACKNOWLEDGEMENTS

Thanks to all the people whose experience with Follow 52 encouraged me to produce this book. Thanks to Cottonwood Church and Christian Fellowship Church, for the opportunity to try out untested ideas. Thanks to Giann and Clarissa for your creativity. And most of all, thanks to Marie, for taking my thoughts and making them much easier for everyone to understand, to better follow Jesus

INTRODUCTION

Following Christ is a walk of grace, but He doesn't leave us on our own to figure out how to live for Him. He gives us clear direction. Follow 52 came out of an experience I had one day when reading the gospels. I came across a command of Jesus in Matthew 25 where Jesus directs His followers to "keep watch." It's clear that Jesus is talking to them about eternity, teaching them what to do today in light of a coming eternity. I understood what Jesus meant by "keep watch," but I had to admit that I didn't actually follow this command. Honestly, I wasn't even sure how to "keep watch" in the 21st century.

This experience made me wonder how many other commands of Jesus gave that I didn't follow. So, I spent the next three months reading through the gospels, over and over again. Every time Jesus gave a command, I wrote it down. The end result was 52 commands written on a piece of paper, every one spoken directly by Christ.

That's when I got the idea to take one command, and each week of the year, do my best to follow that one command. I noticed certain commands were similar, so I organized the commands into monthly themes to help me better follow the commands.

Thousands of people around the world have completed Follow 52. No one succeeds or fails, because Follow 52 is not about performance. It is about the love that we have for God, and since God's love language is obedience, we follow His direction. Follow and learn. Enjoy each week. There may be weeks you don't do so well. Just start again the next week with a new command. Follow 52 is not just following commands. It's following a Person in Jesus. Discover Him each week as you follow Him.

Each week, you will find that space is given for you to record whatever you wish. Also, don't skip over the additional verses. Just one verse can have a huge impact on your understanding and your inspiration to follow Jesus each week. Read one verse each day of that week. Whatever works best for you, commit to do your best to understand and apply the command of Jesus each week so that by the end of each month you will be changed.

#FOLLOW52
Topic 1
Change

Change

People quickly assume that no one likes change, but that is not true. People don't mind change, it's loss they don't like, and change is often associated with loss. If I give a million dollars to someone, their life is going to change, but they are not going to mind those changes. It's only when we see change as loss that we react against change.

Change can mean the loss of security and stability. It can mean the loss of relationship. Change can mean the loss of understanding. But change can also mean new security and greater stability. It can be the development of new relationships and new revelation.

When Jesus commands His followers in this first topic of Change, He is giving us the opportunity to gain what we otherwise would not have. Following Jesus may require that we lose some of life, but the tradeoff is not even comparable.

This month, as you learn how to follow Jesus by making changes to your life, keep focused on the gain you access through Him. Each week, ask for strength to change, and express gratitude that Jesus loves us so much that He doesn't leave us alone, but He helps us change.

CHANGE - WEEK ONE
"Come follow me"
Matthew 4:19

Understanding The Command

Jesus is starting His ministry. He calls His first disciples. He doesn't sign them up for work. He doesn't ask them what they will accomplish for God's Kingdom. He gives them one command: *Come follow me.* If they do this, everything else in their lives will fall into place. Their focus is to follow Christ. As a band of disciples following Jesus, they will watch and learn from Him. They will listen to His teaching, see Him in action, and copy what He does. They will try to do what He teaches.

One thing is clear: Jesus does not want to be merely accepted. He wants to be followed. Jesus is not insecure. He is not looking for people who will "be on his side." He is not looking for people who may applaud Him, yet not join Him. He is looking for people who want to learn how to live in the Kingdom of God from Him. He wants you to follow Him closely, as this command teaches you with three very important words that represent the Follow 52 exercise:

Come: Take the initiative. Following Jesus is not passive.
Follow: You are not in control. You don't set the direction.
Me: This is a relationship. You're following a Person, not a set of rules.

Additional Verses for Study

James 2:17
Deuteronomy 13:4
Psalms 119:60
Matthew 10:38

My Action this Week

Jesus centered His life on people, so to follow His example, this week, identify one person who doesn't always treat you as Jesus would. Every day, pray for that difficult person in your life. Do not avoid that person, but rather, prepare for your interactions with that person this week by asking the question, "How would Jesus handle this interaction? What would Jesus say?" Follow Jesus' example by treating that person the way Jesus would this week. At the end of the week, review how well you followed Jesus' example in your interaction with that person, discovering how you need to grow in your Christ-like character.

What I Discovered this Week

CHANGE - WEEK TWO
"Seek first His Kingdom and His righteousness"
Matthew 6:33

Understanding The Command

Jesus gives this command to improve every part of your life. He instructs you to make seeking Him a priority. The word "first" in Jesus' command does not mean that Jesus is number one before your ten other priorities. It means Jesus is number one, and there is no number two. He is over, in, and through all areas of your life. Your family, your work, and your life are all ways that you seek and follow Him and His kingdom.

Seek is an active verb. You are not to be passive about making Jesus the priority over every area of your life. You are not to compartmentalize your life, thinking that if you give Jesus the first thirty minutes of your day, you can then forget about Him for the other twenty-three and a half hours.

You are to seek His Kingdom and His righteousness in all areas of your life. You are to see His presence and His purpose integrated into every aspect of your life. No part of your life should exist that does not have Christ in it.

Additional Verses for Study

Hebrews 11:6
Proverbs 8:17
Isaiah 55:6-7
Acts 17:24-28

My Action this Week

This week, identify one area of your life where Christ is not present as He should be. Seek Jesus and His Kingdom by figuring out how to involve Christ in that area of your life. It may be with a relationship you have, a hobby, your work, or simply your grocery shopping this week. Whatever it is, figure out how to seek Jesus and His Kingdom first, by making Him a part of that area of your life.

What I Learned this Week

CHANGE - WEEK THREE
"Repent"
Matthew 4:17

Understanding The Command

This command is the foundation you need for following Christ. Without change in your life, you won't follow Christ well. Jesus knew that you would have bad habits, wrong ways of thinking, and personal agendas that don't help you to flourish in God's Kingdom. So He commands you to:

Repent – Following Christ involves identifying areas in your life that are heading in a direction opposite of Jesus and His Kingdom. Then, by His grace and Spirit, you can make the intentional choice to change and move towards Him.

Live in the Kingdom of Heaven – Because of Jesus, and only because of Him, you are able to know and understand the right way. You are not just making a shift to another lifestyle or set of ideas. You are making a shift into another Kingdom in which you were designed to live.

Following Jesus is not just having a saving relationship with God so you can be assured of Heaven, nor is it solely so God can make life on earth better. Following Jesus is about having a relationship with God who moves you to flourish in His divine Kingdom while you live your life on earth.

Additional Verses for Study

Acts 3:19
Romans 2:4
Ezekiel 18:30-32
2 Peter 3:9

My Action this Week

Identify one area of your life where you are living in the opposite direction of the Kingdom of Heaven. This area may be in your values, where your priorities and desires are not in line with Jesus' Kingdom. It may be in your behavior, as you act and speak in ways not in line with Christ. It may be with your beliefs, as you hold on to an idea that is not biblically true. Ask for the Holy Spirit's help each day of the week, as you work on changing by thinking and acting differently.

What I Learned this Week

CHANGE - WEEK FOUR
"Become like the least"
Luke 22:26

Understanding The Command

The disciples are arguing over which of them is the greatest. They aren't even subtle about their pride. Jesus knows that for them to live in the Kingdom of God, and walk in His abundant life, this has to change. Your pride can block you from receiving so much of what God wants to give you. Pride isn't just arrogance. It's a preoccupation with self. Pride is when you only consider things in reference to how they affect you. Pride is when you focus on what people think of you. Pride is when you only put your well being at the center of all decisions. Jesus commands His disciples, which includes you, to change for their own good.

He does this by directing His followers to become least. You should strive to be a servant. In a society driven by the ladder everyone strives to climb, Jesus directs you to put others first, working your way down the ladder. This is a counter-cultural strategy for making life better. By putting others first, you become more like God. By becoming more like God, you are drawn to Him, and become more aware of Him. The disciples were shifting away from God by arguing over who would be greatest. They were doing what God would never do. Jesus teaches all His followers to do what God always does – serve others.

Additional Verses for Study

Philippians 2:1-4
Mark 10:45
Ephesians 6:7-8
Proverbs 11:2

My Action this Week

This week, target people who by society's definition are supposed to serve you, and instead, serve them. Jesus used the analogy of serving at the table, so serve these people in as many practical ways as possible, making their lives better. Each day, find opportunities to serve others, especially those people society says should be serving you. How might you serve the person who bags your groceries? The clerk at the store? An office worker below your rank? Your children? At the end of each day, assess if you served someone, or if you skipped the opportunity to serve. Most importantly, as you serve, pay attention to the condition of your heart.

What I Learned this Week

CHANGE - WEEK FIVE
"Come to me all you who are weary"
Matthew 11:28

Understanding The Command

Everyone gets weary. What do you do when you get really tired? Do you sit on the couch and watch TV? Do you get angry and short-fused? Do you become discouraged? Jesus, knowing you would be weary at times, directs you to come to Him when you find yourself weary. He doesn't tell you to rest. He tells you first to come to Him. He does not instruct you to take a break. You are not given permission to quit what you are doing. These are not solutions to weariness. You are simply told to come to Jesus. Jesus commands you to come to Him with your weariness so He can handle your weariness. What a relief that as a follower of Christ you are not the one who has to manage your weariness.

Jesus' command does not give you a special activity to fix your weariness. This command gives you a special Person who takes on your weariness. Often, when you get weary, it's common to look for a solution or an escape. Jesus instructs you to look for Him. This discipline - to respond to weariness by coming to Jesus - takes practice, as you will be tempted to do so many other things first, like complain, get discouraged, and most of all, do nothing. You need the power of God to start practicing coming to Jesus first.

Additional Verses for Study

Psalm 62:5-7
Philippians 4:19
Exodus 34:21
Psalm 4:8

My Action this Week

Identify where you are weary. Chances are, there will be plenty of options from which to choose. You may be weary with work, with ministry, with family, or a chaotic combination of them all. Once you define your weariness, then come to Jesus. Set aside special time to hang out with Jesus, and find different ways to come to Him with your weariness throughout the week. You can worship Him. You can go for walks with Him. You can abide in His Word. You don't need to do anything radically different this week, you just need to intentionally hand Him your weariness with thanksgiving. At the end of the week, see how you have changed, or better yet, how He has changed you.

What I Learned this Week

#FOLLOW52

Grace

It seems counterintuitive that grace would have commands associated with it. Grace, by its very definition, does not have work. It is a free gift given by God through Jesus. Yet, Jesus wanted His followers to understand this gift of grace, so He gave direction that would position His followers to live in grace.

The commands this month are not commands to receive or achieve grace. They are commands to understand and steward grace in your life. Justice, or even more so, revenge, are common themes in today's world. God's Kingdom, however, is identified by grace. Learning to live in grace is essential to living in God's Kingdom.

A challenge associated with a year long spiritual exercise like Follow 52 is that it can become an exercise of works. Each week, you try your best to obey Jesus, but what started out as an exercise in grace gradually becomes an exercise in proving yourself to Him. That is why this month's commands are so important.

You may want to take communion once or twice this month as part of your exercise, to reflect and reinforce the truth of grace in your walk with Christ. You may want to share Follow 52 this month with friends, as the Bible teaches us that community is a significant resource that enables us to walk in grace. Alone, I default to performance and guilt. With my Christian family, I am constantly reminded of love and grace.

Celebrate grace this month, but also know that you will be challenged to live out grace with others. It's easy to receive grace for our shortcomings. It is much harder to grant grace to others for their shortcomings that make our lives harder. This month, you will discover both how to receive and give grace as you follow Jesus.

GRACE - WEEK SIX
"Forgive 77 times"
Matthew 18:22

Understanding The Command

"How long do I have to put up with this person?" That is the question that Peter asks. It's a question everyone asks. Life has difficult people in it. Life would be easier without the difficult people, so like Peter, everyone asks Jesus how long is required to forgive a hurtful person. Jesus answers by giving a direct command in the form of the number seventy-seven, which means, "always."

Forgiveness is at the center of the Christian faith. God's response to brokenness, pain, and separation is forgiveness. He answers the problem of selfishness in the world with selflessness. This is forgiveness.

To live fully and flourish in your walk with Jesus, you must practice this command to "always forgive." The alternative is to "sometimes not forgive," which is the opposite of God's action to you. He always forgives you. Forgiveness must become as natural to you as breathing. Yes, you need to be wise when you interact with harmful people, but forgiveness in your heart must always be your response to all people. Following Jesus, and learning to forgive, will lead you to discover the richness of His grace in your own life.

Additional Verses for Study

Colossians 3:13
Genesis 50:17
Psalm 130:4
Matthew 6:15

My Action this Week

This week, the application of this command is easy: Forgive every time you are wronged. Do it immediately, and do it always. Sometimes do it out loud, while at other times do it silently. Keep track of how you did, how you felt, and how you discovered His greater grace in your life when you forgave others. And to make sure you don't see yourself as a victim all week, keep track of how often you need to ask others for their forgiveness.

What I Learned this Week

GRACE - WEEK SEVEN
"Leave your gift at the altar and go be reconciled" Matthew 5:24

Understanding The Command

Jesus teaches that reconciliation is a priority for Him and His followers. Before you can worship Him – maybe even in order to be able to worship Him – you must strive for reconciliation.

This command is a high priority to Jesus. It would seem that nothing should trump worship. Yet, here He instructs His followers not just to do something, but when to do it. The priority of this command comes before true worship can take place.

This command teaches you that the purpose of reconciliation is unity, which is the best position from which to worship God. Worship and conflict cannot coexist in God's Kingdom. If you have any kind of unforgiveness in your heart against someone, how can you genuinely go to the Lord and worship Him for the grace you refuse to show others?

This command teaches the practice of reconciliation. Grace and forgiveness are given by God. You cannot create reconciliation, but you are to offer it to others. You must take the initiative to reach out to those who you are separated from, trusting God to work through your actions in order to reconcile with them.

Additional Verses for Study

Romans 12:18
I Corinthians 13:4-5
Colossians 3:12-14
Philippians 2:5

My Action this Week

This week, initiate reconciliation with one person. Don't wait for them to initiate it. Follow Jesus' command and go to them. Go in grace and forgiveness, and try to resolve the conflict. However, also recognize that sometimes you are the one who creates the conflict. When that happens this week, recognize it, admit it, and immediately go to the person to reconcile, asking for forgiveness. Through both forgiving and asking for forgiveness, work at reconciliation this week, prior to your Sunday worship. Then you can come to worship with great expectation.

What I Learned this Week

GRACE - WEEK EIGHT
"Do not judge"
Matthew 7:1

Understanding The Command

This command of Jesus is clear, simple, and straightforward. But what is judging? Is Jesus teaching you to never assess a person or a situation? Are you to eliminate any honest critique? No. When Jesus commands you not to judge, He is speaking about a specific attitude and motivation.

Most of Jesus' commands teach you what to do. This one teaches you what not to do. Jesus knows that judging, for the sake of playing God, will be a temptation in your week. You feel better when you judge others because you compare yourself to them and determine they are not as righteous as you. Judging is wrong when your motivation to judge others comes from insecurity. Judging is detrimental because it enables your flesh to use judging others as a way to lift yourself up. You must not do this. It is harmful to your faith and causes you not to walk in His grace.

Judging others when your desire is to help them, much like a parent needs to judge a child to best direct his or her future, is an important part of being an influential Christian. This command of Christ, to not judge, is an important part of being a Christian of character. Jesus gives you this command to help you be sensitive to the condition of your heart.

Additional Verses for Study

Romans 2:1
Proverbs 21:4
I Corinthians 4:15
James 3:17

My Action this Week

This week, monitor when you are judging people for the purpose of feeling better about yourself. When it happens, ask for forgiveness from God, and remind yourself of His grace in your life. Say a prayer of gratitude for the person you have been judging. Practice the habit of stopping yourself when you are tempted to judge in order to eliminate this temptation from your life of faith and grace.

What I Learned this Week

GRACE - WEEK NINE
"If your brother or sister sins against you, go point out their fault"
Matthew 18:15

Understanding The Command
Relationships that are close and honest will have conflict. Conflict is hard, but it is also an opportunity for reconciliation, which is the visible presentation of the gospel for people. Jesus commands His followers to be bold as an ambassador of His Kingdom in the ministry of reconciliation. When you work at reconciliation, you are giving people a picture of what Jesus has done for them in reconciling them to God.

You are not to go point out someone's faults and show them how wrong they are to exact your revenge and validation. That action on your part gives them a very wrong picture of Jesus. You are to make people aware of His grace for them.

You must see conflict not just as a hardship to be overcome, but as an opportunity for the grace of God to become real in others' lives. It is easier to avoid the person who is "wronging" you than it is to confront them with grace. It sometimes feels better to expose their shortcomings to them rather than forgive them. But you are to go to them for their good, and for yours, to extend grace to them and show them how Jesus loves them.

Additional Verse for Study
Matthew 18:16
Matthew 5:9
Galatians 6:1
Proverbs 10:12

My Action this Week

This week is tough. First, someone will have to wrong you. You can't make that happen, but you cannot avoid hard relationships to protect yourself from being wronged. Then, you will need to meet up with that person who has treated you wrong. You need to pray beforehand and figure out what to say that conveys love and grace, not revenge and hurt. You need to allow the Holy Spirit to work through your words. You may or may not be "wronged" this week, but God may allow it simply for the opportunity to teach you how to follow Him better.

What I Learned this Week

#FOLLOW52
Topic 3
Witness

Witness

Many have found this month to be one of the most challenging and rewarding months for Follow 52. Being a witness of Jesus in public to others is scary. Knowing what to say, when to say it, and how to say it isn't even the hardest part. For some reason, making people aware of our faith in Christ, and their need for Christ, comes with a lot of fear and anxiety.

Jesus knew that we would be at our best when we overcame our fears and began to be more honest with our identity. To be a Christ follower is who you are. To be in relationship with others and not be honest with who you are, is not being yourself. So this month, more than anything, you will learn to be true to yourself as you witness who Jesus is to you.

Part of this month is about our spiritual transformation, but part of this month is about gaining a practical skill. Everyone has a story, and like the woman at the well, we need to learn how to tell our story to our village. Identify three talking points to your story with Jesus that makes it easy to share with others. Practice telling your story to others. Start with those who make it easy for you to share. Then, once you're comfortable telling your story, move on to others who do not know you as a Christ-follower.

This month, you have the chance to face a fear, and with the power of the Holy Spirit, experience a conquest of that fear. You'll learn that the fear was actually unfounded, once you make the intentional choice to be a witness of Jesus Christ to others. Take the opportunity this month gives you to open a new dimension of your faith and your walk with Jesus.

WITNESS - WEEK TEN
"Let your light shine before others"
Matthew 5:16

Understanding The Command
Jesus assumes His followers are doing good and that they already have light. He commands you to do good so that His light will shine on others. This command has to do with the influence you have on others through your actions and words as a follower of Christ:

Let - You should not do anything that hinders light from shining. You need to position yourself with people. Light is no benefit to others if you are so removed from people that they are not able to see the light in you.

Shine - Light is attractive. It creates a visible awareness. Your light should be easily seen and have a positive impact as it shines on others.

Others - Everyone needs to see God's goodness. It is not enough for you to only show your good deeds to Christians. You need to show your good deeds in life to others who don't know Christ, so they see Christ through your actions and words.

You are to enable everyone to see God's goodness. Following Christ includes positioning yourself in the world, through your good actions and uplifting words, so people can see the love of God.

Additional Verses for Study
I Peter 2:9
Daniel 12:3
Ephesians 6:18-20
I Corinthians 10:31

My Action this Week

Let your light shine on someone by doing an intentional act of kindness. Then, along with the act of kindness, use your words to tell that person about the love of Christ. Use your actions to serve, and your words to explain (rather than merely actions without explanation). For you to follow this command best, the person needs to be someone not close to you, so they can see Jesus. Jesus does not ask you to recruit people to His Kingdom. He asks you to let His light that is in you intentionally shine on people.

What I Learned this Week

WITNESS - WEEK ELEVEN
"You must testify"
John 15:27

Understanding The Command
Often, Jesus' command for your life is also helpful to someone else's life. With this command, Jesus directs you to tell others what He has done for you. It is for your own good to speak out, yet it is for the good of others to hear your story.

People will not believe without hearing. You will believe even more when you speak out. Your testimony is a partnership with the Holy Spirit of God. Jesus teaches that the Spirit of God will testify and you will also testify. This gives your words incredible power and influence beyond your earthly ability.

It is not your skill as a public speaker that makes you an effective witness. It is the genuine testimony of God in your life that comes across so powerfully and genuinely to others. Don't complicate this command. Just tell your story.

This is the easiest of commands, yet the hardest. Staying silent seems so much safer than speaking out. What if you say the wrong thing? What if you're ridiculed for your faith? What if you don't have answers? All these questions are irrelevant to Jesus' command. He does not command you to teach a college class, give a lecture, or debate an atheist. He only directs you to tell your story. Leave the rest to Him.

Additional Verses for Study
Acts 1:8
Psalm 40:9-10
I Corinthians 9:19-23
I Peter 3:15

My Action this Week

This week, tell the story of your relationship with Jesus to one person.

What I Learned this Week

WITNESS - WEEK TWELVE
"Go home and tell how much the Lord has done for you"
Mark 5:19

Understanding The Command
Jesus commands the man in this passage not to be so consumed with following Him that he stops sharing Christ with others. This is good for you to know. Jesus gives the man (and you) direction:

Go home - Start telling people about Jesus with whom you already have a relationship.

Tell them - Be specific and clear. You are not selling them anything. You are not debating them. You are telling a story of the Lord's work in your life.

How much the Lord has done - Talk about what the Lord has done, not the condition of the people. Make God the center of discussion, not politics, morality, or anything else.

When you simply tell the story of how good the Lord has been to you, He takes care of everything else.

Additional Verse for Study
Isaiah 63:7
Romans 1:16
Acts 16:14-15
2 Corinthians 5:20

My Action this Week

Identify one person in your extended family who is distant from God. Take that person out for a meal, genuinely showing interest. Tell them what God has done for you. In preparation for telling your story, pray and ask God for the best words to describe His goodness in your life.

What I Learned this Week

WITNESS - WEEK THIRTEEN
"Go out two by two"
Mark 6:7

Understanding The Command

Christianity is always about the group, the family, the body. Jesus wants His followers to do nothing alone. He often commands His followers to "go out," but this week's command brings more clarity to "going out." Don't go out alone. In order to effectively follow Jesus' command to "go out," you must be in community, for you can only go out with others who share your faith.

Following Jesus is about reaching others with the love of Christ. It is also about joining a community of faith. This command connects these two major aspects together. You are called to His church and you are called to His world. Going out two by two is how Jesus links both dimensions of your faith: To be in a community of faith, yet also be an influence in the world. When you follow this command, you are truly living fully in His design.

The number of people going out together, in this case "two," is not to be legalistically applied, but it does reflect an intimacy and support for each other. Jesus is asking you to join with a few brothers and sisters, reaching people relationally.

Additional Verse for Study

2 Timothy 1:8
Isaiah 6:8
Matthew 18:20
Hebrews 10:24

My Action this Week

Invite a Christian friend to join you on an "outreach activity." The specific activity is not important. What matters is that you do this with Christian friends, going out together, relying on and supporting each other, as you reach your community. Together, you may volunteer at a soup kitchen, or you may share Christ with people. What matters most is that you will do this together.

What I Learned this Week

#FOLLOW52
Topic 4
FINANCES

Finances

Jesus' commands are all spiritual. This month, He addresses an area of our lives that has such a tremendous impact on us spiritually. Finances are personal and private. No one asks and no one tells others about their financial situation. Jesus goes against common culture by making finances not a personal practical matter, but by directing His followers to see their finances as deeply spiritual.

Everyone has his or her own position on the topic of money. Jesus had His position on the topic as well. He didn't address every detail about money in our daily lives, but He did address the details that He considered most important. His teachings should determine how we handle money in our daily lives. Follow 52 is not designed to debate issues. It is designed to help us to practice what Jesus taught. Focus on the act of obedience this month more than debating the topic of money.

If you are already following Jesus when it comes to money, don't think because it's Follow 52 you have to do more than continue to follow the command. Be happy that you are already following Jesus by giving to Him. For some, Follow 52 this month will be an affirmation of what is already happening. For others, it may be quite challenging.

My experience has been that giving happens when you make a commitment to it regularly. Giving is both a practice and a spirit. Jesus teaches through His commands that giving needs to be done in a certain way and with a certain attitude. Let this month be a month of honest reflection. You may hide your practice and attitude about money from others, but don't hide it from Jesus. Let Him help you this month.

FINANCES - WEEK FOURTEEN
"Store up for yourselves treasures in heaven"
Matthew 6:20

Understanding The Command

Jesus teaches on the act of investing. He instructs you to invest in a way that gives you an eternal return on your investment. This directive from Jesus could be applied to many different resources in which you invest: time, energy, money, relationships. It may be easiest for learning to follow Jesus to apply it to money.

The key is to focus on the outcome of heaven. Life is not to be designed to be lived with only the temporary in mind. Society compels you to act and invest with the goal of immediate gratification. People make decisions around money, time, and relationships wanting the benefit today. This command keeps your mind, heart, and attention where it needs to be, on eternity.

Every good investor knows that timing is everything. Jesus, the smartest investor to walk this earth, gives you the timing you need to guide your investments in life. In society, waiting is bad. But in His Kingdom, waiting is good. Good stuff happens to those who wait. Great stuff happens when you invest in eternity and wait for that return on investment. And in light of eternity, it's actually not that long of a wait, because in comparison, the years on earth are but the blink of an eye.

Additional Verses for Study

Proverbs 13:16
Luke 14:28-30
Proverbs 14:29
Matthew 19:21

My Action this Week

This week, identify three ways you can "store up treasure in heaven," knowing that you may not see a return on your investment this side of eternity. Here are some ideas:

1) Give an additional offering for Kingdom work
2) Help someone grow in their faith
3) Spend extra time in prayer

The point of your action is to simply make a statement to Jesus and to yourself that you will measure your investment in life by eternity.

What I Learned this Week

FINANCES - WEEK FIFTEEN
"Give back to God what is God's"
Matthew 22:21

Understanding The Command

Jesus teaches a great deal with this one command. First, He teaches that He does not want you to hold back from God what rightfully belongs to God. Why? Because it is in your best interest not to hold on to that which does not belong to you. The Bible teaches that the first 10% of your income (called the tithe, which literally means 10%) is what you are to give back to God.

Second, Jesus teaches that it is your responsibility to initiate this return. God will not forcefully take it back. You must give it. Why? Because it gives you the opportunity to show your faith and loyalty to Him. If He took it, like garnishing wages, you would have no option. God gives you the choice to follow Him.

Third, Jesus teaches that you have been given a great deal from God. You are only giving back to God a small portion of so much more that He has given you. The rest you get to keep. But you always need to remember that all you have comes from Him. Giving back 10% is a form of worship and trust in God as your Provider.

Rather than calling your action "giving," maybe it is more accurate to call it "returning," for He is the one who keeps "giving" you so much more.

Additional Verses for Study

Proverbs 3:9-10
Malachi 3:10
Genesis 14:19-20
Hebrews 7:1-2

My Action this Week

This week, tithe; give 10% of your weekly income to your local church. You may already follow this command each week, so this week, when you give in the offering, remember the word "return" and gratefully acknowledge that God is really the Giver in this relationship.

What I Learned this Week

FINANCES - WEEK SIXTEEN
"When you give to the needy do not let your left hand know what your right hand is doing"
Matthew 6:3

Understanding The Command

This command seems impossible to follow. How do you give and yet not know you are giving? Jesus is giving a hyperbolic teaching, but a command nonetheless. He wants you to be more than discreet in your giving. He wants you to be absent in some way. Your giving must be absent of your ego, your ability, and your reward. You are present in faith, but your focus must be on Christ. Without Christ, you have nothing to give. You are only able to give because of Christ. Choose to give because of Christ.

Christ gives this command to protect you. When you don't focus on your ability in giving, then you are protected from focusing on yourself and losing sight of true faith and glory in giving. When you focus on yourself with giving, then you see yourself either as a hero or as a victim. For example, if you give a lot of money you are a hero, but if you don't give much, you are a victim, blaming your lack on other factors beyond your control. In both scenarios you put yourself at the center. Jesus wants to protect you by instructing you to remove yourself from the center of giving.

You are neither a hero nor a victim when it comes to your giving. You are a faithful, grateful follower of Christ who recognizes everything you have comes from Him. You work hard and manage well, but He is the Provider of all you have.

Additional Verses for Study

Ecclesiastes 5:10
Hebrews 13:5
1 Timothy 6:10
1 Corinthians 16:1-2

My Action this Week

This is a unique command to try to follow, but here are a few ideas. Each time you give, make a declaration about Christ as your source. Each time you give, make sure no one else knows about it. Each time you give, say a prayer of gratitude. Each time you give, if you have a thought that puts yourself in the center of your giving, acknowledge the wrong thought and remove it from your mind.

What I Learned this Week

FINANCES - WEEK SEVENTEEN
"Use worldly wealth to gain friends for yourselves" Luke 16:9

Understanding The Command

This command can seem strange without the story that accompanies it. Jesus taught a parable of a manager whose future is in doubt, so he uses his money to secure friends who will take care of him when he gets fired. Jesus contrasts the manager with His disciples, showing them how much wiser the manager was in handling his money than the disciples were in handling God's money.

Christ-followers should be the wisest people on the planet with money. Jesus instructs His disciples to use their resources to reach people for eternity. These people will welcome them into their reward in eternity. Money is meant for Kingdom use. The Kingdom is people. Jesus wants you to be wise and see your money as a means for helping people. These people are your children, your family, your neighbors, and even lost people on the other side of the globe who you will not know until eternity.

This parable and command teaches you how to look at money. Money is a valuable resource. It provides for you and your family, but more than that, it creates a bridge of relationship. People, especially those in need, need friends who can help them. You don't help them by buying their friendship. You help them, as a result of Christ's love, knowing that through the friendship you can show them Christ's love.

Additional Verses for Study

Acts 4:34
Psalm 37:16-17
Deuteronomy 15:7
Proverbs 13:11

My Action this Week

This week, make a financial investment for the purpose of reaching people with the gospel. Use the wealth of the world that God has given you to reach people for eternity. Give enough to stretch yourself, perhaps an additional 10% of your week's income. Invest in eternity like a wise manager of God's money.

What I Learned this Week

#FOLLOW52

Topic 5
CHARACTER

Character

Character is not just about our behavior, but about our heart and mind. How we believe and think ultimately is revealed by how we act. Many of Jesus' commands this month will address your heart and mind more than simply your actions.

However, if there ever was a month for Follow 52 to be misinterpreted, resulting in guilt and shame, this is that month. Grace is what enables us to follow Jesus. As you learn and follow Jesus' commands on character, it is probably this month that you will struggle, and struggles in following Jesus can make us feel "unsuccessful," resulting in guilt and shame.

Do not let the enemy or anyone deceive you. Jesus delights in you. The fact that you would take on a yearlong exercise just to be nearer to Him, and live in a way that honors Him, brings Him great blessing. No one grows at something without having to work at it.

Character is about who we are, especially on the inside, but it has a public dimension to it. Before you can fully walk in the grace and love of Jesus, you have to acknowledge that you care about how others see your spirituality, and that at times you act religiously in order to influence their view of you. Start from that honest position of humility and this month will be an amazing discovery of His love for you.

You have an opportunity this month to do some honest reflection. Make sure to write down your thoughts each week. Often God speaks to us and shows us a truth, but if we don't record it the busyness of life causes us to forget what we discovered. As you follow Jesus this month, take time to make note of what He is teaching you.

CHARACTER - WEEK EIGHTEEN
"Do not swear an oath"
Matthew 5:34

Understanding The Command

Words matter. They matter greatly. They are a window into the heart. How you speak and interact with people determines so much of your life. So Jesus directs you to be very careful with what you say, especially when it comes to "swearing an oath." He teaches you how to speak and how not to speak.

Swearing an oath is how people would convince others they were going to fulfill a promise. Jesus wants your words to be truthful and reliable. There should be no need for an oath to convince others and persuade them. Your words need to simply be true and honest. Also, Jesus wants your words to have no confusion or ambiguity. Let your yes be yes, and your no be no. Jesus is directing you not to make statements that are untrue, or even unclear.

This is one simple, yet hard, lesson for many. You need to speak the truth, clearly and honestly. If you are telling the truth, you don't need to swear on a Bible. You don't need to persuade. Speaking clearly also at times means knowing when to stay silent if your words will not be clear and honest. For example, when you are tempted to defend yourself against unfair criticism, it may be better to stay quiet until you find the clear and honest words to speak. Your character and your words have a strong connection to each other. Jesus starts you off this month by commanding you to be very attentive to your words.

Additional Verses for Study

James 5:12
Colossians 4:6
Proverbs 18:21
Ephesians 4:29

My Action this Week

This week, pay close attention to your conversations. First, do not swear an oath, meaning only speak the clear truth, not trying to convince someone manipulatively. Second, be aware of when you need to be silent if your words are going to create confusion and be misleading.

What I Learned this Week

CHARACTER - WEEK NINETEEN
"If your hand or foot causes you to stumble, cut it off" Matthew 18:8

Understanding The Command

Whoa! Cut off a hand?! Seriously? How are you to follow this command, and what does Jesus mean by it? If you were to literally obey Jesus, how many body parts would you have left? Yet, we don't want to water down Christ's teaching either. There is a reason why He uses such an extreme example.

Jesus is teaching to live life in full view of others. He teaches that you should not let your life mislead people away from God. Jesus wants you to eliminate anything in your life that would cause others to be distracted away from God because of you.

What might cause you to mislead others? The lack of spiritual integrity (not living what you claim to believe) can cause others to be cynical towards God and Christianity. And in a moment of weakness, you can say or do something that will influence someone to stumble and sin, and lead them away from God.

Jesus wants you to take great care and attention to the idea that your life influences other people. You are to influence them towards God, not away from Him. You are supposed to draw people to God, not away from Him. Anything that gets in the way of getting closer to God needs to be removed so your influence will honor God.

Additional Verses for Study

Ephesians 4:27
Psalms 94:18
I John 4:4
Romans 6:12-14

My Action this Week

It is easy to make excuses for some activities in your life that are not drawing you to God, and may be leading others away from God as well. This week, eliminate one activity or habit from your life, because it hinders you from walking strong in Jesus and influencing others toward Him.

What I Learned this Week

CHARACTER - WEEK TWENTY
"See to it that the light within you is not darkness"
Luke 11:35

Understanding The Command

This is another tough command. Jesus is teaching you about what you should be putting into your life, and what you should not be putting into your life. As a Christian, you regularly assess your Christian behavior. You examine how you're doing. But often you look at the end result, but don't always examine the process that gets you to the end result. Jesus wants you to look seriously at the process of building a Christ-following identity.

He wants you to take a hard look at what you put into your life. His command is simple. Don't let darkness in. You can claim to have light in you, but there truly may be some darkness in you, if that is what you have been putting in yourself. How does this practically work? For example, if you have conflict with someone and allow bitterness and unforgiveness to take root, then you are allowing darkness to enter into your life. Your Christian identity is damaged by what you allow into your life.

This is a simple command to understand: Don't let any darkness in. It is a much harder command to follow.

Additional Verses for Study

2 Timothy 2:15
Matthew 23:27
Psalm 139:23-24
I John 1:9

My Action this Week

At the end of each day this week, do a review and see if there were any situations where you allowed darkness to creep into your life. Darkness often comes in the form of wrong thoughts and wrong influences. At the end of the week, take that list and burn it, signifying God's grace that saves and empowers you. Burning the list will also signify your commitment to eliminate any entry points of darkness into your life.

What I Learned this Week

CHARACTER - WEEK TWENTY-ONE
"Watch out for the yeast of the Pharisees"
Mark 8:15

Understanding The Command

Yeast is a small ingredient, yet when mixed with a larger ingredient, it has the power to change the very nature of that larger ingredient. Through this metaphor, Jesus is teaching four important truths when following Him:

1. You don't need much yeast for it to affect your life.
2. The impact of a small amount of yeast can be very bad for you.
3. Yeast is what religious people possess.
4. You are susceptible to get this yeast in your life.

So what is this yeast? The yeast of the Pharisees can be described in various ways. It can be defined as any religious identity you take on to prove yourself spiritually valid to others. When you do that, you replace the grace of God with this religious identity. Even just a small amount of that yeast will spread to every other area of your walk with Jesus. So He warns you to watch out for it.

This command is a command of awareness. Don't be naive. The possibility of replacing grace in your spiritual walk with your own spiritual ability is very real. If you are aware of it, you are halfway there to being protected. If you disregard it, you are susceptible to its subtle, yet strong, urge to make you look more spiritual to others.

Additional Verses for Study

Ephesians 2:8-9
Galatians 2:16
John 8:1-11
I Corinthians 15:33

My Action this Week
This week, meet with a close friend and give them permission to tell you any areas where there are "seeds" of this yeast that urge you to prove your spirituality. When these seeds of yeast are identified, be humble enough to accept the truth. Confess it and let God's grace strengthen you. Then, watch out for it in the future as you continue to walk in God's grace!

What I Learned this Week

CHARACTER - WEEK TWENTY-TWO
"Stop sinning"
John 5:14

Understanding The Command

Clear. Simple. Honest. But seemingly impossible! How are you to stop sinning? What is Jesus commanding you to do? Jesus teaches the man that it is God who heals him, but then He warns the man that if he keeps sinning, he positions himself for continued bad consequences. You are saved by grace and healed by God. But salvation today doesn't exempt you from the consequences of your choices.

Stop sinning. Everyone sins. Some have sinful habits as a lifestyle, and all have sinful acts that are done in a moment of weakness. While you are learning to follow Jesus, you will continue, at times, to behave wrongly. But you can also continue to grow, eliminating sinful acts from your life as you rely on the power of the Holy Spirit and God's church to help you grow into a mature Christ-follower.

Stop sinning. Although your primary focus as a Christ follower is to seek God, there is a place in following Jesus for addressing sin and doing what needs to be done to stop the bad choices in your life.

Additional Verses for Study

Ephesians 5:1-4
Romans 6:23
I Corinthians 10:13
James 4:17

My Action this Week

You don't need a revelation from heaven, or even much reflection, to know you sin. This week, address your sin. First, tell someone about your sin so you can walk in His grace and have accountability to overcome it. Second, find a trigger that enables you to be strong in faith when you face temptation. Third, increase your time with the Holy Spirit so that by His power you can stop sinning. Just pick one area to work on this week, learning to overcome your sin through the power of the Holy Spirit and with intentional effort.

What I Learned this Week

#FOLLOW52
Topic 6
SERVANTHOOD

Servanthood

We all want to be in control of our lives. We want to be the masters of our own domain. But when we do, we make our lives harder and more painful than they need to be. That is why this month's topic of servanthood is so important.

Jesus told His followers that He came not to be served, but to serve. Servanthood is one of the key characteristics of Christ. This creates a dilemma, as self-centeredness is one of the key characteristics of life today. We are bombarded with messages to live free to be ourselves. Jesus lived His life to serve others. This month will require some very honest self-reflection from you. If you are willing to do this, you will discover a new dimension of Jesus' character in your life.

Jesus gives commands, not just for the present, but for the future. Servanthood is often for the future. Jesus teaches us how to treat other people, knowing the result it will bring for the future, as well as for the present. People don't change overnight. But if you trust Jesus and follow His way, the commands of servanthood are essential for how to influence and help people change for the better.

As difficult and counter-intuitive as servanthood may seem, this month may be the most rewarding month in your yearlong Follow 52 exercise. Being a servant can have immediate reward as people respond gratefully and favorably to being served. However, not all people respond that way. No matter how people respond, follow Jesus' commands to serve as an act of obedience to Him, and not to the people you are serving.

We are a servant in identity to Him. We serve people because of who we are in Christ. With or without an immediate sense of reward for serving people, this month will show you a significant part of your identity in Christ.

SERVANTHOOD - WEEK TWENTY-THREE
"Take up your cross"
Mark 8:34

Understanding The Command

You cannot die the death Jesus died, but you can strive to live the life Jesus lived. Jesus describes the life you are to live by commanding you to center your life in the identity of the cross. Life is not meant to be designed with the goal of comfort and convenience, but with the reality of service. When you die to self to live for others, you become most like Christ.

Jesus gives this command to shape your values and attitude towards life and people. The cross is not just an event you observe; it's an event you participate in. In Galatians chapter two Paul said, "I have been crucified with Christ so now the life I live I live by faith in the Son of God." If you are going to live for Jesus, you must see the cross as central to your life. Taking up your cross has many diverse applications regardless of your life situation. But if you don't start with the condition of your heart, the application will simply become religious obligation.

If you are to copy the life of Jesus, following every aspect of Him, then you must trust Him and go against the pattern of society. The greatest life to live is serving others, because it is a life that is most like Jesus.

Additional Verses for Study

Hebrews 6:10
Romans 12:1
1 Samuel 12:24
John 12:26

My Action this Week

This week, intensify your attitude and value in "taking up my cross." First, study additional passages in the Bible on taking up your cross to fully understand the truth. Then, pray everyday to the Holy Spirit to create in you a heart that "takes up the cross." Finally, trust that God will present you with one practical opportunity this week to take up your cross, applying this command to make the value even deeper in your heart.

What I Learned this Week

SERVANTHOOD - WEEK TWENTY-FOUR
"Do to others what you would have them do to you"
Matthew 7:12

Understanding The Command
This command is proactive, preventative, and passionate.

It is proactive in that you don't wait for people to treat you well so you know how to respond to them. If you wait, then you will only be nice to people who are nice to you, and rude to people who are rude to you. Jesus helps you by directing you to take initiative in treating people not based on their treatment of you, but based on how you want to be treated.

It is preventative because if you treat people how you want to be treated, there is a good probability that they will respond in the same way that you have treated them. You get to greatly influence the nature of the relationship you have with them. This may not happen overnight, but eventually people respond in the same way they are treated.

It is passionate because your treatment of people is defined by how you want to be treated. There is a principle of sowing and reaping in this command. If people are treating you wrong, you need to examine how you are treating them and trust that following Jesus will bring about a change in your interaction.

Additional Verses for Study
Ephesians 5:21
Galatians 5:13
1 Peter 4:10
Mark 10:42-45

My Action this Week

Every morning, make note of one person you will interact with on that day. Be intentional, led by the Holy Spirit, in determining how you will treat them (based on how you want to be treated). You may not see immediate changes in them, but keep treating people correctly, believing that change will take place in the future.

What I Learned this Week

SERVANTHOOD - WEEK TWENTY-FIVE
"Have salt among yourselves"
Mark 9:50

Understanding The Command

Jesus uses the idea of salt in diverse ways. Salt preserves and purifies. Salt is also used as a metaphor for being an influence in the world. But at the end of this teaching, He uses salt for a slightly different meaning when He commands His followers to have "salt among yourselves." Salt was used as a means of establishing a covenant between individuals. Numbers 8:19, 2 Chronicles 13:5, and Leviticus 2:13 all mention a covenant of salt.

Jesus is talking to His disciples who are arguing about which one of them would be greatest. He wants them to be servants to each other. He knows that they will only work best as a team and only represent the Kingdom best if they serve each other. So He draws on this covenant theme of salt to teach them about their relationship in the Kingdom.

Jesus gives you the same directive. You are to be salt with others in the Body of Christ. You are to serve and always remember that part of your covenant with God means that you are in a covenant with Christians as well. The strongest application of that covenant is to serve them. Christianity is not just serving the world, but serving fellow believers.

Additional Verses for Study

Matthew 23:11
1 Chronicles 28:9
2 Chronicles 13:5
Hebrews 9:14

My Action this Week

This week, you can best apply this command by serving someone close to you, like your spouse. You should find many ways to serve this person. What is important is that he or she not ask, but that you initiate the serving. It is also important that you truly help the person, not just serve as you normally would do. In serving this person uniquely and proactively, you reinforce the "covenant of salt" you have with Jesus.

What I Learned this Week

SERVANTHOOD - WEEK TWENTY-SIX
"Be one"
John 17:21

Understanding The Command

Every Christian knows that unity in the church is important. But what is often forgotten is that when Jesus commands the church to "be one," He is making a far deeper spiritual directive.

Jesus is directing you to be one with others, the same way He is one in the Trinity with the Father and the Holy Spirit. As a member of the Body of Christ, you are to reflect that same unity with other Christians. The Oneness of the Trinity is characterized, for example, by deflecting attention away from self, and drawing it to others. The Father expresses how wonderful His Son is. The Son says He does nothing unless directed by the Father. The Holy Spirit points everyone to Jesus. Each member champions the other.

To follow Jesus' command for unity is not merely being tolerant of other Christians. He directs you to work and build a unity in the church that is deeply spiritual, reflecting the Trinity of God. When the church reflects the unity of God to the world, something divine takes place. Jesus ends His prayer stating that if the church fulfill this command to "be one," then the world will know who He is and what He has done for them. You, along with all others, have a specific role to play in the world knowing God.

Additional Verses for Study

1 Corinthians 1:10
Colossians 3:14
Ephesians 4:3
Psalms 133:1

My Action this Week

This week, initiate actions with others that reflect the unity of the Trinity. Champion someone else. Sacrifice for someone else. Join together with someone else for a Kingdom cause. Do this with your family (especially your children, if applicable) or with your church family.

What I Learned this Week

#FOLLOW52
Topic 7
FAITH

Faith

This month, we follow Jesus' commands that directly relate to faith. Faith is not just an emotion or a theology. Faith is an action. It is a choice you and I make about the role we will allow Jesus to play in our lives. May this month be a month where Jesus is more present than ever as you act in faith.

Following Jesus in faith could take all year of this spiritual exercise, and in some ways, faith is woven into each month of learning to follow Him. Take this month and really commit to it, but without the burden of performance. Without faith it is impossible to please God. Jesus wants you trusting Him the way He trusts you. He does not want you performing for Him.

Sometimes, humor helps when doing Follow 52. Without faith, there is anxiety and worry. Consider who Jesus is and all that He has done for you, and ask yourself why you're worried. I don't mean to make light of whatever situation is causing you worry. Just try easing your exercise this month with a lighthearted approach.

Also, the Bible teaches us to accompany our faith with confession. Speaking out loud makes a thought far more real and honest. Find a good friend that you can speak to this month about how you are believing and how you struggle to believe. Talk to someone as you follow Jesus' command.

Jesus knew that faith is like a muscle which can either grow or atrophy. He gave specific commands to have the muscle of faith grow in His followers so they could live victorious lives, sometimes in the face of great adversity. This is a month for you to grow and get stronger!

FAITH - WEEK TWENTY-SEVEN
"Don't be afraid, just believe"
Mark 5:36

Understanding The Command

Fear is a common response to the unknown. Faith is the other option available for you to take. Faith may not fully eliminate fear, but it can overpower it. If you believe, and act on what you believe, then fear cannot rule your life. Fear will always be present, but you can use fear for good, as it will remind you to choose faith.

But faith does not just happen. It takes practice. You must live each day, choosing to trust God and His Word. You will then see your faith grow. Faith is not an event. Faith is a lifestyle, with actions reflecting your lifestyle choice each day.

Thankfully, God's acceptance of you is not based on your faith, but His grace. Your acceptance of Him, however, is based on faith. You must choose to trust Him. There is no better option.

Additional Verses for Study

Ephesians 3:20-21
1 Peter 1:21
1 John 5:4
Revelation 21:1-5

My Action this Week

This week, identify one area of your life where you have fear. It may be in sharing your faith in Christ to strangers. It may be regarding your finances, or a task you don't feel capable of doing. Counteract your fear this week with an act of faith. Invite a neighbor to church, or give a larger donation than usual, or take on a challenging task. Whatever the case, do an act of faith that will override your fear.

What I Learned this Week

FAITH - WEEK TWENTY-EIGHT
"Do not worry"
Luke 12:22

Understanding The Command

This command seems silly. Nobody wants to worry. Worry is not an act of disobedience that you are eager to commit. You don't get up each morning ready to face the day with worry. Yet, Jesus knew you would worry, so He is direct in His command. Worry is not to be accepted as a regular part of your life as a Christ-follower.

Worry is a fruitless and destructive practice. Worry never helps. It does not put your mind at ease. It does not give you wisdom for right choices. It increases anxiety and skews your perspective on reality. It makes sense that Jesus directs you not to make worry part of your routine in facing life's challenges.

The key to not worrying is to find a replacement for when you are tempted to worry. If you don't worry, you need something else to do in its place. Each time you want to worry, worship instead. You can, with thanksgiving, present your situation to God and trust Him with it, but you must begin by choosing to eliminate worry from your life.

Additional Verses for Study

James 2:17
Deuteronomy 13:4
Psalms 119:60
Matthew 10:38

My Action this Week

This week, practice not worrying with a simple response each time you worry. Each time worry enters your mind, stop and give thanks to God for who He is in response to your worry. If you worry about money, worship Him for being your Provider. If you worry about health, worship Him for being your Healer. If you worry about a relationship, worship Him for being a Prince of Peace. Each time you start to worry, replace your worry with worship and give thanks to God for who He is.

What I Learned this Week

FAITH - WEEK TWENTY-NINE
"Come follow me"
Matthew 4:19

Understanding The Command

Do you really trust Jesus? Trust comes before evidence. Before you see the change you need in your life, you must believe Jesus will bring about that change. Trust also remains even after the evidence, because trust is relational. Faith is not a magical code only needed for results. Faith is how you relate to Jesus. You trust Him, and He trusts you.

Jesus requires that your relationship with Him be based on trust. He directs you to trust Him and not merely the evidence of His activity. His evidence is all around. It would be easy to base your relationship on His activity, but He wants you to base your relationship with Him on trust. You must continue to believe for more of Jesus in your life and never be settled with all that you already see He has given you.

Faith in Christ means a life of submission. You trust His way. You trust His activity. You trust His future for you. More than anything, you trust His character. You believe you have received because of who He is, and after you receive what you are asking Jesus for, you continue to live trusting Him.

Additional Verses for Study

Romans 1:17
Romans 10:9-10
Ephesians 3:16-19
Matthew 17:20

My Action this Week

This week, follow Jesus' command by acting on what you are trusting Jesus for, believing you have received it. For example, if you are trusting Jesus to restore a relationship, then act in grace to that person. If you are trusting Jesus to provide for a financial need, then give generously and gratefully. Act in faith. Do not be foolish or presumptuous, but neither should you wait until all the natural evidence is present for you to see, before you thank Him for His faithfulness in your life.

What I Learned this Week

FAITH - WEEK THIRTY
"Do not let your hearts be troubled"
John 14:1

Understanding The Command

Jesus knew that "troubled hearts" would be part of life on this earth. He directs you with this command, but He also gives you a great encouragement. His command teaches you that you determine what you allow the condition of your heart to become. "Do not let" means that you have the power in Christ to "not allow" whatever is troubling you to negatively affect your life.

Without your intentional action, your heart will become troubled. You have to protect and guard your heart from what could happen without your activity. This command is one of prevention. Commands are easier to follow when they have an immediate gain. You are probably more apt to obey when you can see the result of your obedience right away. However, this command is a directive from Jesus for your future.

If you engage in habits to protect and guard your heart today, then in the future, your heart will not be troubled. You need to obey today, knowing that the payoff comes tomorrow.

Additional Verses for Study

Hebrews 11:1-40
Proverbs 12:25
Proverbs 17:22
Psalms 43:5

My Action this Week

A troubled heart often comes from despair and worry. How do you guard against this? With gratitude and worship. This week, make a list, adding to it each day, of all the good things Jesus has done for you that day. Spend time each evening thanking God for His goodness. Guard your heart by filling it with worship and gratitude for the goodness of God.

What I Learned this Week

#FOLLOW52
Topic 8
DEVOTION

Devotion

Jesus taught His followers how to engage in a relationship with God. This is what devotion is all about. Devotion requires a desire of the heart. However, Jesus also taught that devotion requires a specific way for the heart to express itself. We aren't left alone to figure out how to relate to God. Jesus taught us how to act on the desires of our heart.

God created humankind holistically. Body, soul, mind, spirit, and heart are all woven together. Fasting, communion, prayer, and other devotional practices are all important ways that our material selves and our immaterial selves connect together.

Jesus knew that we would need to exercise our faith in order for it to grow. Devotion is the workout that causes faith to grow. Devotion is usually defined by what we do. We engage in various devotional habits to seek God. These are good and beneficial.

Devotion is more than just reading your Bible and praying each day. Those practices really matter and add great value to a relationship with Christ, but devotion is a position you take in life that defines what really matters to you, or in this case, who really matters to you.

DEVOTION - WEEK THIRTY-ONE
"When you pray, go into your room and close the door."
Matthew 6:6

Understanding The Command

Jesus is teaching His disciples how to pray. He is very practical in His command. Jesus knew that many of His followers, for centuries to come, would struggle with a consistent prayer habit. We start and then stop. Our day gets too busy and we don't make time. When we are discouraged, and don't feel like praying, we allow our emotions to dictate our actions.

So Jesus gives us clear direction to do two things to help us pray more effectively. First, go into a room. You need to have a location that you identify as your place of prayer. When you have a set location, it helps you create a regular habit.

Second, Jesus directs you to close the door. You need to pray when and where there are no distractions. You are not to pray in panic or chaos. You need to find the right time when your heart and mind can focus on your prayer with God.

Jesus is not interested in the religious ritual of prayer. He knows that effective prayer, as devotion in your life, takes place through good practices which create good habits. Habits turn into lifestyles.

Additional Verses for Study

I John 5:14
I Corinthians 6:11
Ephesians 6:18
Jeremiah 29:12

My Action this Week

This week, establish a habit at the same time and same location in order to exercise your devotion of prayer. You could go on a prayer walk each morning, or pray every afternoon during your lunch break. No matter what you choose, make the intentional effort to spend time in devotion with God, building your faith.

What I Learned this Week

DEVOTION - WEEK THIRTY-TWO
"When you pray, say Father...."
Luke 11:2

Understanding The Command

Jesus doesn't tell you to pray. With this instructive command, Jesus assumes that you're already praying, so He teaches you how to do it. Jesus teaches on prayer often, giving various directions on how to pray. This command is about the object of your prayer.

When you pray, you are to go to your Heavenly Father. Jesus is not legalistic in prayer, demanding that only the Father is to be addressed in every prayer. However, addressing your Father God in prayer is very important. Praying to the Father gives you an important insight into what prayer is designed to be.

Prayer is a means of relationship. It is a dialogue. But it is more than a conversation, because prayer results in change, both situational and personal. When you pray, things change. More importantly, when you pray, you change. All of this happens because of your Heavenly Father.

Jesus knew it would be tempting for us to make prayer into a magical chant with the sole purpose of only changing our circumstances. If we did that, we wouldn't care who made the changes happen, whether it was Santa Claus, a Higher Power, or luck. As long as things changed, it wouldn't matter, but for the Christ-follower, the who of prayer matters even more than the what of prayer.

Additional Verses for Study

I Thessalonians 5:16-18
I John 5:14-15
2 Chronicles 7:14
Proverbs 15:29

My Action this Week

This week, be intentional in praying to your Heavenly Father. Pray with the purpose of relationship. Speak to your Father as a child, and listen to your Father. Focus your faith primarily on the love and power of your Father, instead of only wanting your circumstance to be changed. Pray, giving specific attention to Who you are addressing.

What I Learned this Week

DEVOTION - WEEK THIRTY-THREE
"When you fast, put oil on your head."
Matthew 6:17

Understanding The Command

Again, Jesus assumes His followers are fasting. Fasting was a regular habit for Jewish people. It had, and still has, both spiritual and physical benefits when done correctly. Here, Jesus gives a command on how to fast correctly for the spiritual benefit of the person fasting.

Fasting is an act that is meant to separate you from the world. You deny your flesh what it desires, and in doing so, you remove yourself from being desire-driven. This denial provides a unique opportunity before God. You can hear from Him clearly. You can draw close to Him intimately. But with this unique position of fasting comes the temptation of pride. This is what Jesus' command addresses.

Jesus instructs you to show yourself in public in such a way that no one will know you are fasting. He instructs this to protect you. He knows the temptation you will face. He knows how others may judge you because of your fast, so when you fast, Jesus teaches you to "hide it." He directs you not to let anyone know you're fasting.

You are not to lie about fasting, but you are to be proactive in presenting yourself so no one is aware of your fasting. You should not show your fasting as a means of portraying your great spiritual ability and maturity.

Additional Verses for Study

Acts 14:23
Joel 2:12-13
Esther 4:16
Daniel 9:3-4

My Action this Week

In order to obey Jesus' command this week, you must fast. You must choose to fast from something that can be hidden from others. You can fast from food and not let anyone know. If food is too challenging, you can fast from other things, like social media, but even then you must find ways to hide your fasting. This week, remove yourself from a desire and draw yourself to God, yet do it privately, so you are protected from spiritual pride.

What I Learned this Week

DEVOTION - WEEK THIRTY-FOUR
"Take and eat; this is my Body. Drink, this is my blood." Matthew 26:26-28

Understanding The Command

Jesus commands that you take communion. He commands this because He wants you to always remember Him in a specific way. Jesus is so intentional in leading you that He even directs you on how you are to remember Him. He guides you in how to define your relationship with Him. He doesn't leave it up to you to decide how to relate to Him.

Jesus wants you to remember Him in what seems to be His weakest moment. Jesus gave amazing, life-changing teachings. He did supernatural miracles. He showed amazing compassion. Yet, He wants you to remember Him in the moment of His death. He wants you to remember not just what He did for others, but what He did for you.

This command may be the most loving command ever given by Jesus. Commands by nature are authoritative. Commands direct. Commands tell us what to do to complete a task. Yet, this command to take communion tells the story of love and sacrifice. It tells you what Jesus did, so you don't have to do anything. You are commanded to always remember His love and His sacrifice. You are never allowed to move away from Jesus and His cross. This command should humble us, yet we should be so very grateful to follow it.

Additional Verses for Study

Luke 22:19-20
I Corinthians 11:23-27
I Corinthians 11:28-29
I Chronicles 16:15

My Action this Week

This week, take communion. Take it at church, or take it with your family. Whichever way you take communion, do not take it as a religious ritual with merely symbolic meaning. Instead, take communion as a genuine spiritual exercise, following the command of Jesus, and discovering more of who He is to you.

What I Learned this Week

DEVOTION - WEEK THIRTY-FIVE
"Consider carefully how you listen."
Luke 8:18

Understanding The Command

Jesus gives this command after teaching His followers a parable about a sower who plants seed on different types of soil. Yet, it's an unusual command as ultimately He instructs you to be a good listener. A listener is a receiver. Jesus is teaching you to be intentional as a recipient of His Word.

This command challenges your intentionality and practice as a listener. You can be too quick in hearing His Word (shallow soil), too stubborn (hard soil), or too selfish (weedy soil). Or, you can be attentive and alert (fertile soil), ready to receive whatever He wants to tell you. Jesus does not force His truth on you. You have a role in receiving His truth. The soil of your heart matters when receiving God's truth.

To be a good listener, you must be prepared to listen. Your heart must be readied. If you are in a hurry, or in a bad mood, or having a pity party, you will not listen well. And if you don't listen well, you will not receive His Word well. This week, Jesus commands you to prepare yourself for one of His greatest gifts - His Word.

Additional Verses for Study

James 1:19
Psalm 46:10
Revelation 3:20
Job 11:13

My Action this Week

Each day this week, before you read your Bible, spend a few minutes preparing your heart so that you can consider carefully how you listen. You can pray, or have someone pray for you. You can listen to worship first before listening to His Word. You can simply stop, breathe and clear your mind before listening. Also, prepare the soil of your heart before going to church. Each day, judge your condition, and change the soil of your heart to listen well.

What I Learned this Week

#FOLLOW52
Topic 9
MISSION

Mission

Jesus spoke quite a bit about mission during His three years of ministry. We already had the theme of Witness, but Mission is different. Mission addresses the larger purpose God has on this earth with His creation. We have an important role in the bigger picture, just as we have an important role in witnessing our faith to individuals. As you go through these next four weeks, you have the opportunity to discover God's purpose for you within His purpose for the world.

The commands of Jesus concerning mission are some of His best known commands. They are taught, and even recited, often in churches. Yet, in some ways, it is still hard for us to apply these commands into our lives individually. Don't over-spiritualize and overcomplicate the mission commands of Jesus. You don't have to move to another country. These commands challenge you to start habits in your life that you can practice for years to come.

If you have any success with the commands of Christ on mission, then you may experience fallout from people. Being a Christian means that we will face opposition. Our values and our mission stands in contrast to the values and ways of the society we live in. Jesus knew this. He forewarned us about this. And He gives commands on how to live in grace and love, even when facing difficulty for being a Christian on mission with God.

MISSION - WEEK THIRTY-SIX
"Ask the Lord of the harvest to send out workers." Matthew 9:38

Understanding The Command

This command is unique in that Jesus directs you to speak to God about a specific issue. He is teaching you how to pray. He is giving you the content for your prayer. Jesus knows that in His command to you is a promise that transforms your life in God's Kingdom.

Jesus instructs you specifically in your role for the expansion of His Kingdom. There are many options He gives for helping build His Kingdom, but in this one thing, you do not have a choice. You are instructed to partner with God to see His Church mobilized for His Kingdom. Why does Jesus command you to pray?

If you pray, you change. You see yourself as one of those who are "sent." Your prayer for workers for the harvest results in you becoming an answer to that very prayer. Furthermore, when you pray for workers to be sent, you realize that you are not alone in going into the world. You are part of a grace-carrying army. Finally, this prayer makes you more humble and at peace. It helps you remember that He is in charge of the expansion of His Kingdom. Our response should be one of gratitude, grateful to be a worker for Him, joining all His other workers.

Additional Verses for Study

Ephesians 2:10
Psalms 96:3
Isaiah 52:7
Acts 13:2-3

My Action this Week

Each day this week, ask God to send out workers. Your prayer can focus on the type of work (missions, compassion, justice, evangelism) and the type of worker needed for that kind of Kingdom work. Or, simply pray for all workers. As you pray for God to send out workers, reflect and listen to Him as He asks you to join His workers in being sent into the harvest.

What I Learned this Week

MISSION - WEEK THIRTY-SEVEN
"Invite the poor, crippled, lame and blind to a banquet."
Luke 14:13

Understanding The Command

Jesus gives a specific command as an action item which reflects the identity you are to have as a Christ follower. God's Kingdom places great value and priority on the broken and the outcast. In one sense, you are, like everyone else in His Kingdom, a poor and crippled person, but Jesus may not simply be speaking metaphorically here. Jesus is teaching you that God's banquet table is especially set for those who rarely get invited to anything else.

In contrast to society where invitations are based on an individual's importance, or determined by by wealth, power, fame, or status, in God's Kingdom the guests of honor are those who seem the least important in this world. In God's world, they carry great importance; they carry great value.

Jesus commands you to act towards them now as if you are already living fully with them in God's Kingdom for eternity. Obeying Jesus' command is not merely telling them about the gospel. It is inviting these hurting, poor people into your life and your world. Jesus is commanding you to make your life a place where they are welcome. Don't do this as a hero, but as a servant, learning from them as you serve them.

Additional Verses for Study

Hebrews 13:2
Isaiah 58:7
Galatians 6:2
Proverbs 19:17

My Action this Week

If you don't already have a relationship with people that society devalues, this week you will ask God to identify someone who is poor and broken. Invite them into your life so they can experience firsthand the value and importance God places on them. You can take them out to eat. You can spend time with them. Give them an invitation to God's banquet, through Jesus, delivered by you with grace and dignity.

What I Learned this Week

MISSION - WEEK THIRTY-EIGHT
"Go and make disciples of all nations."
Matthew 28:19

Understanding The Command

Jesus enlists you into His service on the front lines of His Kingdom work. He directs you to do what He Himself did. This command is not based on your gifting, ability, or your position of influence. This command is for you and for everyone who calls themselves a follower of Christ.

It is critical to your identity that you play a part in seeing His Kingdom established by helping people become devoted followers of Christ. Making a disciple of Christ does not mean getting people to follow a moral code. Neither does it mean simply getting people to say the sinners' prayer. Making a disciple of Christ is about having your relationships include a dimension where you are guiding friends in their relationship with Jesus Christ.

Jesus added a geographic location to His command. He is not explicitly telling you that you must go to every nation. You are not required to travel to every country to be obedient, but you also can't just stay among your own people. You are directed by Christ to live a life that crosses cultural and ethnic barriers. You are to play a role in all nations having the opportunity to become disciples of Christ. All are welcome. You must reflect this value to the world.

Additional Verses for Study

Romans 10:13-14
I Chronicles 16:24
Psalms 105:1
2 Timothy 2:2

My Action this Week

It takes far longer than one week to fulfill this command, but this week, you can take an important first step in following Jesus' command to make disciples. The first step is to "go." You must be the one who adds a spiritual dimension to your relationship with friends. This week, take your relationship with one of your friends into a Kingdom dimension, helping him or her become a disciple of Jesus.

What I Learned this Week

MISSION - WEEK THIRTY-NINE
"Pray for those who persecute you."
Matthew 5:44

Understanding The Command

This command is not much different from another command Jesus gave when He said, "Love your enemies." But this command is more specific in that it directs you in one very important way to love and bless those who are against you.

Jesus instructs you to pray for those who are against you because of your faith in Christ, because He loves them as much as He loves you. If He didn't love them, He would teach you to avoid them. But He does love them, and He knows that your prayers matter, for them and for you. He instructs you to pray, so that your heart will be guarded, and so bitterness will not take root in your heart against those who hurt you. Often, we are tempted to avoid or attack those who persecute us instead of praying for them. If you do this, it will destroy you from the inside out. Jesus is protecting you with this simple and direct command. Your prayers must include those who come against you because of your faith.

Jesus wants your relationship with them, which at first is defined by separation and brokenness, to be a story of reconciliation and healing. So He directs you to pray. The gospel is a message of reconciliation. You have been made an ambassador of reconciliation. Persecution and separation are the perfect opportunity to present the gospel in its living message. When you pray for those who are against you, the gospel comes alive in you. You are better equipped to love them. You become a living message of God's love and reconciliation for them.

Additional Verses for Study

1 Thessalonians 2:13-14
Proverbs 25:21-22
Galatians 6:9
I Thessalonians 2:4

My Action this Week

This week, make a list of people who treat you badly at times because of your stand as a Christian. This list can include people directly in your life as well as those who persecute your brothers and sisters around the world. Pray every day for people who are persecuting the church, and in doing so, are persecuting Jesus Himself. Strive to pray with understanding so you will also learn more about the persecuted church this week. Watch as your prayer changes you.

What I Learned this Week

#FOLLOW52
Topic 10
SEEK

Seek

The idea of seeking after God is throughout both the Old and New Testament. Paul considered everything a loss compared to knowing and pursuing Jesus. Commit this topic to be a topic of heart change. Life distracts us easily, and we lose sight of what really matters. Through His commands, Jesus wants to remind us that seeking Him is the highest priority for our lives.

In order to seek, we must be honest with ourselves. Seeking demands self-reflection. We have to ask ourselves: In what areas of our lives do we allow fear to stop us from seeking Jesus? Sometimes, self-reflection is easier when we share our fears and questions with a trusted friend. We are called to seek together.

Sometimes, the commands of Jesus are not specific actions for a specific day; the commands related to seeking are like this at times. Of course, there are ways we can seek Christ each day, but seeking refers more to how we define the values in our lives. Society tries to influence us with its set of values. Jesus, with His command to seek Him, wants to help us set our values for life. As you learn to follow Jesus through seeking, take time to think about your life, not just your daily actions, and let Jesus shape who you are to become.

Seeking enables us to be aware of the bigger cosmic reality that exists beyond our earthly situations. Jesus' command to seek Him challenges us to not merely live earthly lives that follow Him; we are to live eternally-minded lives.

SEEK - WEEK FORTY
"Ask. Seek. Knock."
Matthew 7:7

Understanding The Command

Through this command, Jesus gives you permission to approach your Father in heaven with a request. Jesus directs you to never hesitate in coming to God. This command makes it clear to you that God wants you to come before Him, always and for all things.

Ask - You can be clear in your requests. You don't need to be ambiguous. Honesty with God is the best form of communication, as long as you communicate humbly.

Seek - You can pursue God. Don't just bring your requests to Him; pursue Him personally through your requests. Don't just desire answers to your needs, but also more of God revealed to you.

Knock - You can be confident. Don't come before Him groveling or with doubt and fear. He is your loving Father. His love for you gives you a confidence to come boldly before the throne of God.

Additional Verses for Study

Matthew 13:44-46
Psalms 27:8
I Chronicles 16:11
Psalms 14:2

My Action this Week

Each day this week, come before God. Let your prayer be clear and practical (ask). Have your prayer include a desire for revelation (seek). When you pray, speak with faith and confidence (knock). This week, pray according to this pattern that Jesus commands.

What I Learned this Week

SEEK - WEEK FORTY-ONE
"Get out of the boat and come to me."
Matthew 14:29

Understanding The Command

Jesus is speaking to Peter, but His command has direct application to your life. To get out of the boat is to remove yourself from any place in life that provides you with a false sense of security. Jesus is not in the boat. Jesus is not in your false sense of security. You must leave your false place of security and bring any fear you have to Jesus. It is not enough to get out of the boat. You must go to Jesus with your fear, allow Him to remove it, and trust in Him.

Your fear may be insecurity in your identity, panic about money issues, or fear of failure. If so, your false sense of security may cause you to avoid people. Your panic over money may cause you to totally control your money and never give it to God. Your fear of failure my keep you from trying something new and cause you to miss amazing adventures with God. These fears and attempts at self-made security do not work. They do not bring peace and comfort. They are false and do not eliminate fear.

Bringing your fear to Jesus is the only way you can address your fears. But to do that, you must first recognize the false way in which you have been dealing with your fears and remove yourself from those ways. You must get out of the boat and go to Him. You must trust Jesus with your money. You must engage in relationships where people will get to know you. You must try something new that carries the possibility of failure. When you do this, you are getting out of the boat and coming to Jesus.

Additional Verses for Study

2 Thessalonians 3:5
I Chronicles 28:9
Psalms 27:4
Psalms 119:2

My Action this Week

This week, identify one place where you hold on to a false sense of security and release yourself from that place and bring your fear to Jesus. Ask a good friend for their insight into areas where you are not looking to Jesus. Come up with tangible actions to "get out of the boat" and bring your fear to Jesus.

What I Learned this Week

SEEK - WEEK FORTY-TWO
"Remain in me."
John 15:4

Understanding The Command

This is a very broad, and yet very simple, command. It is broad because it speaks to every part of your life, yet it is simple because it gives you one goal for your life. You are to never be disconnected from Jesus. You are to remain in Him, in every season of life.

Jesus uses the illustration of the vine and branches when giving this command. This illustration gives you insight into the application of this command. The branches draw life and nourishment from the vine, just as you are to draw life and nourishment from Jesus. He is your source of life. When you look to other things as life-giving, you begin to no longer remain in Him. For example, you can look to your career or a relationship to give you life.

Of course, Jesus wants your work and relationships to be meaningful to you, but not replace His role as the main source of life. Rather than segregate Jesus from daily life, this commands directs you to integrate Jesus into all aspects of your daily life. You can best remain in Jesus when He is part of your work and part of your relationships.

Additional Verses for Study

II John 1:9
Mark 1:35
John 8:31
Colossians 2:6

My Action this Week

This week, find ways to integrate Jesus into your work life and your relationships so you can remain in Him. Share your faith with a co-worker. Tell a story of how Jesus has brought you life to a friend. Remain in Him by making Him part of your daily life this week.

What I Learned this Week

SEEK - WEEK FORTY-THREE
"Keep watch."
Matthew 24:42

Understanding The Command

Jesus does not want you to be unaware of the reality of His return. He wants you to live each day fully aware that your time on earth is not the sum total of your life. Jesus does not want you to be lulled into believing that your temporary, earthly life has greater meaning than your eternal life.

Your life is to be defined by the eternal. His command to "keep watch" is a simple actionable item that helps you keep your life defined by eternity. There is a greater story and a greater timeline being played out for you and for the world. You need to be aware of this, so Jesus commands you to keep watch.

The Bible teaches that no one knows the exact details of God's eternal timeline. Keeping watch is not a command to look into a crystal ball and guess God's timing. Keeping watch is to be aware of your life in the scope of eternity.

Additional Verses for Study

Colossians 3:1-2
Deuteronomy 4:29-31
Proverbs 28:5
Zephaniah 2:3

My Action this Week

To fulfill this command, you will need to study portions of scripture, like Revelation and Daniel. Pray eternally minded. Make or review your financial investment strategy. You can't do all this in a week, but this week you can make a plan. You can plan how in the months to come you can live more fully aware of God's eternity at work right now.

What I Learned this Week

#FOLLOW52
Topic 11
COMPASSION

Compassion

Jesus was very well known for the amazing compassion He had for people. Jesus went against tradition by having compassion for the people His society rejected. He touched lepers. He held children. He spoke to women. For this topic, focus your efforts of compassion towards those people our society rejects.

The commands of compassion cannot be obeyed if you do not have relationships with other people. God's design is that every Christian be a part of a Christian community, a local church. Some Christians attend a weekend service, but they are not really a part of the community. If that is you, realize that you are missing out on some rich blessings. To follow Jesus in extending compassion requires that you be part of a church. When you commit to fully becoming a part of a church, following Jesus gets much easier.

Compassion requires relationships. If you are trying to follow Jesus alone, you are robbing people of the gift God has made you to be for them. You are a gift, and people are a gift to you. Obey His command to be compassionate to others by seeing yourself as a gift to others.

SEEK - WEEK FORTY-FOUR
"Let the children come to me."
Matthew 19:14

Understanding The Command

Jesus loved the weak and the vulnerable. Children had no place in most religious environments during His time on earth. Jesus commands His disciples to allow the children, who represent those disregarded because they are weak and vulnerable, to have direct access to Him.

Jesus changes the way in which you see and measure people's value. First, you need to see these people as valuable. Secondly, your job is to make a way for the weak and vulnerable to come to Jesus. This is part of your leadership role as a Christ-follower. You are to help those who may struggle in coming to Jesus on their own.

Jesus does want all to come to Him, but in this command He is not only directing the disciples metaphorically. Jesus actually wants children to come to Him. You are directed to live out His Kingdom priority of children.

Additional Verses for Study

Deuteronomy 6:6-7
Proverbs 22:6
Ephesians 6:4
1 John 3:1

My Action this Week

This week, help children discover and see Jesus. If you have small children this will be easier for you, but if you do not have children, or your children are adults, find a creative way to help children discover Jesus this week. You could link up with a family to help their children discover Jesus. You could help at a children's event. You could begin to sponsor a child through Compassion International and write to that child about Jesus. There are many options available for you to follow Jesus in this command.

What I Learned this Week

COMPASSION - WEEK FORTY-FIVE
"You give them something to eat."
Matthew 14:16

Understanding The Command

Jesus commands you to help people. Specifically, in this context, He commands His disciples to join Him in providing food for people. You are directed by Jesus to be a part of God's work in providing for people's physical needs. You are not just to pay for people to have food. You are to help people get their physical needs met.

Jesus' command requires a hands on approach, and that is important. He knows that when you do the work itself, it puts you in contact with needy people and you are challenged to show them true love. If you only make a donation to feed people, you are able to stay removed from them. Their hardship does not touch you and affect you. But when you are the one handing them food, you're truly impacted by their pain.

Jesus never wants compassion to be an act of distance. It is always an act of intimacy. God has supernaturally given to you, so you in turn can give to others. Because of God, you can provide for them. Because of God, you can love them with His love. You can give them more than you could ever give them on your own because of Christ in you.

Additional Verses for Study

Isaiah 58:10
Isaiah 49:10
Lamentations 3:32
I John 3:17-18

My Action this Week

This week, engage in an act of compassion to help someone in a tangible way with their physical needs. To fully obey Jesus' command, you need to do the work itself by faith in Christ, in a way that enables you to touch the people. This will cause you to grow in your trust of Jesus to provide for their needs, and genuinely show them His love through you.

What I Learned this Week

COMPASSION - WEEK FORTY-SIX
"Go and have mercy on people."
Luke 10:37

Understanding The Command

People have so many needs. Some needs are physical, while other needs are emotional and spiritual. Often, giving mercy to people is categorized as spiritual and emotional ministry. But Jesus gives this command after telling the parable of the Good Samaritan.

This parable is a story of a person in great physical need. Yet the command at the end is to have mercy. Jesus is teaching that mercy and caring for people's physical needs are not unrelated. Being merciful is giving someone who is dying of thirst a drink of life-giving water. Having mercy is helping someone who otherwise cannot help themselves.

Mercy is to be given to people, regardless of their status or qualifications. Mercy is given because he or she is your neighbor. You need to see hurting people. You need to understand who the true enemy is and know that people can change when God works through you. As you have mercy on them and care for them, they can be healed. Having mercy begins with how you see people, and continues with how you treat them.

Additional Verses for Study

Colossians 3:12
Exodus 33:19
Daniel 9:9
Isaiah 63:7

My Action this Week

This week, find one person who needs mercy. It may be someone who has treated you wrong, or simply a neighbor who is struggling. See him or her with the eyes and heart of mercy, but do more than just see that person. Help that person as a tangible expression of mercy.

What I Learned this Week

COMPASSION - WEEK FORTY-SEVEN
"Give to the one who asks you."
Matthew 5:42

Understanding The Command

This seems like a risky command. If anyone asks me, am I to just give to them freely because I am obeying Jesus? Doesn't that mean that I can be taken advantage of?

Jesus is not making a random command. This command is part of a larger teaching where Jesus teaches how to live as a follower of Christ with others. You are called by Jesus to be generous and giving in your relationships. You are to have a heart to help others, rather than setting up protection for yourself.

When you are asked for help, your immediate response should be to figure out a way to help that person. Rather than carefully measuring the cost to you, your first response should be to see how you can help and answer their request. You can give time. You can give resource. You can give faith and encouragement. When someone asks, you are to be ready to respond and give.

Additional Verses for Study

Deuteronomy 16:17
1 Peter 3:8
Galatians 6:2
Hebrews 13:16

My Action this Week

This week, every instance someone asks you for something, respond. Do not hesitate to weigh the sacrifice. Do not protect yourself. Do not think about it too much. Simply put, if asked, do it. This week, take the risk to go out of your way to help others to see what Jesus does through your obedience rather than just playing it safe.

What I Learned this Week

COMPASSION - WEEK FORTY-EIGHT
"Take care of my sheep."
John 21:16

Understanding The Command

Jesus wants your focus to be on loving people. He does not need you to be a hero for His cause. He does not need you to be highly specialized. He only asks you to love and care for people.

His sheep are the family of Christ, His Church. People need taking care of. No one can survive alone. And when one sheep wanders off, then that sheep is in danger of an enemy coming in for the kill. Jesus gives you a simple and clear command: Take care of people so they will be safe.

Sometimes, you may feel pressure like you must do great things for Jesus. You may be frustrated at the smallness of your life. But this command sets all that aside. Jesus does not want you to feel pressure. He does not expect you to perform successfully for Him. All Jesus asks is that you care for people. If you do this, He takes care of the rest. Jesus counts by ones, and He directs you to care for people, one by one.

Additional Verses for Study

2 Corinthians 1:3-4
James 1:27
Zechariah 7:10
Philippians 2:4

My Action this Week

This week, identify someone in your church who needs help in some way and care for them. Whether it is a physical, spiritual, or emotional need, care for them. Especially look for anyone who is alone so that your care for them will help bring them back into the flock.

What I Learned this Week

#FOLLOW52
Topic 12
LOVE

Love

The theme of Love is fitting for the final topic of Follow 52. We didn't take on this challenge to prove ourselves. We did it only because God loves us and we love Him, and God's love language is obedience.

This topic is wonderful and difficult. Jesus teaches about how to manage our enemies, yet many of us don't have enemies. We are challenged as to how boldly we really do live out our faith. Jesus teaches us to love unconditionally, and that is easy until we get hurt by others. Be as honest as you can with yourself during this topic. His command to love can radically change your life as a Christ-follower. It won't be easy, but it will be transformational.

Jesus' commands to love has great popularity, but not as much obedience. Everyone knows the story of Jesus washing His disciples feet, yet not everyone follows through on His command to do the same. Everyone knows the teaching of turning the other cheek, but often we keep our heads stiff.

During this final topic of Follow 52, take time to see all the other commands in light of this month's topic of Love. When asked to summarize all the law, Jesus said, "Love God and love others." Take time while following Jesus in this topic of love to reflect on all His commands.

LOVE - WEEK FORTY-NINE
"Love your neighbor as yourself."
Matthew 22:39

Understanding The Command

This is a strange command. Christianity is supposed to be a selfless religion. Yet, Jesus directs you to use yourself as the standard for the love that you will give to others. How does this work and why would He give such a command?

Loving yourself isn't selfish. When you love yourself, you are accepting Christ's love for you. And that is how you are to love your neighbor. Just as you accept Christ's unconditional love for yourself, you also need to be a vessel of Christ's unconditional love for your neighbors. You need to love them just as you are loved by God.

Through this command, Jesus is teaching you how to love people. Your neighbor is part of your life. Your neighbor is your family. Your neighbor is a part of the family of God. There is no separation between God's love for you and God's love for your neighbor. So if God doesn't separate that love, neither should you. You need to love your neighbor just as you are loved by God.

Additional Verses for Study

Romans 15:2
1 John 4:19
1 John 4:21
James 2:8

My Action this Week

This week, identify one neighbor - a family member, church member, or a genuine neighbor - and love them as you love yourself. Love them with the same unconditional love that Christ shows you. Pray that through your love they will discover more of Christ's love.

What I Learned this Week

LOVE - WEEK FIFTY
"Love your enemies."
Matthew 5:44

Understanding The Command

Do you have enemies? Perhaps you have shielded your life too much from people. Although some people truly are enemies of God and His Kingdom, at times we don't really experience them as "our" personal enemies.

How do you get enemies? You can't go out looking for them. You can't hire enemies. But yet, Jesus commands you to love your enemies, as if He expects that you will have them. A Christ-following lifestyle is loving, but it is also divisive. Darkness cannot tolerate light. When you shine brightly, you will gain enemies.

This command teaches you indirectly that your light needs to shine more brightly. You need to speak the truth in love more assertively. You need to work in places where your light will confront darkness. And when you do confront darkness and you're persecuted for it, your response needs to be love. If your response is not rooted in love, how else can your enemy be saved?

Additional Verses for Study

Romans 12:19-21
Proverbs 24:17-20
1 Thessalonians 3:12-13
Luke 23:34

My Action this Week

This week, go out as a light intently into darkness. You can do this at work, with a family member, or in your community. Then, you need to be prepared to show love for your enemy in a very tangible way. Surprise your enemy with a battle tactic that does not destroy them, but with one that rescues them by love.

What I Learned this Week

LOVE - WEEK FIFTY-ONE
"Wash one another's feet."
John 13:14

Understanding The Command

This command is the ultimate act of servanthood. This was an act only done by a servant. Jesus takes a servant's job and makes it deeply spiritual. Jesus makes all of His followers uncomfortable with this act. His disciples do not want to be a part of it.

This type of spiritual service often gets the same response from us today. At times, when we serve people, we want to do it as a hero, not as a servant. We want to come in with money, care, or expertise and "save the day" for them. We don't want to serve people as a servant. It humbles us and positions us below others. On the surface it seems to show us as weak when we want to come across as strong. We can find ourselves willing to serve, but not in a vulnerable way. At times, we can want to serve from a position of strength over the person.

Jesus commands you to serve from a position of humility below the person. I can see why the disciples reacted against this command. But this command gives you a great blessing. It keeps you in the position of a servant. It protects you from ever thinking you are the Master. You not only serve people, but you do so as a servant, not as a master.

Additional Verses for Study

1 Corinthians 16:14
Proverbs 11:25
1 Corinthians 11:1
James 3:13

My Action this Week

This week, wash someone else's feet by not just helping someone, but by serving them from a position of humility. How do you do this? It starts in your heart. Do not see yourself as a hero, but simply as a servant of Christ. Second, serve quietly, even anonymously if possible. Third, give all glory to God for the ability to serve others. Ask the Lord to give you a task of service that makes you into a humble servant.

What I Learned this Week

LOVE - WEEK FIFTY-TWO
"Love the Lord your God with all your heart, soul and mind."
Matthew 22:37

Understanding The Command
This is a command from Jesus to you, to love God. Is it possible to command someone to love someone else? Doesn't there need to be some emotion or will involved? You can follow a command to give or to serve, but to love? How does this command work?

Jesus is directing you *how* to love God, more than commanding you *to* love God. Jesus teaches in this command that if you are to truly love God, your actions must have very particular characteristics.

To love God must be all-encompassing. Loving God is not an occasional pursuit. You are to love God with ALL of your heart, soul, and mind. These three aspects that define your total existence are to be fully in love with God. Your heart is with your complete passion. Your soul is your identity. And your mind is with your knowledge. They work together in showing that loving God is not one-dimensional. He loves you wholly and you are to love Him wholly.

Additional Verses for Study
1 Corinthians 13:13
1 John 4:7
1 John 3:16-18
Psalms 18:1

My Action this Week

This week, identify a specific way to love God with your heart, your soul, and your mind. Love God from the depth of your emotion, perhaps by worshiping Him in nature. Love God out of your identity, with service to others. Finally, love God by discovering more of Him by studying His Word.

What I Learned this Week

ABOUT THE AUTHOR

Joel Holm is a follower of Christ, a life-long learner, and a compulsive, creative thinker. He has a passion to help people to know and live in truth. He has earned two Masters degrees, traveled to more than 90 countries, and written numerous books. From his vast and unique global experiences, Joel brings a wealth of knowledge and learning. He has a keen insight into God's Word as it applies to Christians living in the 21st century. Joel is most grateful that he gets to share his adventurous life with his wife, Marie.

Made in the USA
Las Vegas, NV
05 January 2021